A fi

ISBN: 978-1-913642-34-1   2nd Edition

The author has asserted their right to be identified as the author of this Work in accordance with the Copyright, Designs and Patents Act 1988

Book designed by Aaron Kent

Edited by Aaron Kent

Broken Sleep Books (2021), Talgarreg, Wales

Contents

Stravaig

David Wheatley

Dramatis personae

AISLING, young woman.
HECTOR, rural gent.
ARTHUR, middle-aged man.
MRS MCGILLIVRAY, religious enthusiast.
EILIDH, jogger.
PERCY, toddler.
SADHBH, child in arms.
BOY, passer-by.

SCENE: rural Aberdeenshire.

[*Sound of pram wheels and the opening bars, piano part only, of Schubert's 'Der Leiermann', giving way to distant wind chimes.*]

AISLING: The chimes, the chimes, baby Sadhbh! I hear their tinny music from over the lochans, tossed this way and that on the breeze. If you stand and listen you might fancy they were playing your song. [*Sings.*] 'Up a bogey lane, to buy a penny whistle, a bogey man came up to me…' Foolish fancy. But when all you hear, all day, is your mother's voice, perhaps all voices melt into my voice, all melt into one. [*Baby gurgles.*] For you, I mean. [*Baby gurgles.*] And for me too, the sound of my voice tossed and returned to me on the breeze. [*Pause.*] Now, is it this or the next turn. Dalmadilly, land of the… whortleberry. Whortleberries, to put on your porridge, baby Sadhbh! But where is that father of yours, off at his Pictish stones again. An 'incomparable recumbent', he said, just past the woods. Perhaps he is taking a rubbing of the inscription. Lovely day for it though, to disappear down a back lane between the high hedges. And what sharp heat, as sharp as the spikes on the gorse. But will he have remembered to water the boy… the *bairn*, though, I wonder. And will the youngster have a clean bottom? Imagine how an unchanged load in his nappy would chafe the poor thing, baby Sadhbh, and your Daddy so forgetful, with his mind on his bits of old rock. Granite, gabbro or norite: just saying the names is ever so cosy, and the touch of my boy's fingers trailed along the moss in search of a ladybird or a beetle… But is that a ladybird on your hand, baby Sadhbh? Let me count the spots… [*Sound of a passing van.*] What's that curse o' God… [*Mumbles.*] Well bless us and save us, it's farmer Finlay's lorry on its way to market this fine morning! Can you see the poor sheep reaching their snouts out the side? Is it for shearing they're being taken, or… the other thing? It was just the other month the lambs were slipping on their placentas wherever you looked, and look at them now! The grown sheep I mean, unless it's their mothers he's transporting, or both. [*Pause.*] Merrily off to slaughter. [*Pause.*] Of course they feel nothing, they'd have you believe. [*Emphatic.*] There'll be no meat eaten in the house and you growing up, baby Sadhbh! But what have I done to save the wee beasties, their poor tongues hanging from their drouthy mouths? And farmer Finlay reached a hand out the window, too, as he passed, in salutation. [*Vehement.*] I should rebuff him angrily, the puce-faced old brute. He shoots crows too, you know, I've seen them hanging from his fence. [*Baby gurgles. Calmer.*] What terrors await our heedless neighbours, baby Sadhbh when our mask of civility slips. [*Cackles.*] Terrors, I say. [*Pause. A gust of wind.*] But what's that blowing across my face? Why, it's may blossom, stripped from the trees and strewing the road before us. Consider it a good omen. Unlike those malevolent crows – craws – up ahead. I see you! Some birds scurry and others hop, why is that. [*Pause.*] Even collecting carrion, crossing the road to a juicy disaster left in the wake of a passing lorry, they hop. [*Pause.*] Rather than trudge, trudge-push, push. [*Pause.*] The swing from season to season here is savage, baby Sadhbh, simply savage. Tonight I will watch the last of the evening light disappear through the curtains behind Millstone Hill at almost eleven, yet six months ago 'darkness was the universe', as the poet said, and will be again. Just as you were making your appearance. How we hunkered – bunkered – down together through those Arctic nights. My little seed of light, sprouting into our difficult spring and now this unending summer-long daylight! How to reconcile these extremes we hurtle between, hurtle-trudge. I cannot. All I can do is push the wheels round from moment to moment. You are my load and yet it is you who spirit me along, so uncomplainingly too. [*Baby gurgles.*] And on we go to the garden centre, with our menfolk lurking somewhere *en route*. How will young Percy hail us though: yesterday it was [*adopts child's voice*] 'I saw an octagon, Mammy'. Precocious soul. He meant a stop sign. Of course it's all parroting, really, but what am I but a parrot too, turning my jabberings over on my tongue like sweets someone else has sucked first. And yet when I ask him, 'who am I Percy, what's Mammy's name', he will say nothing. Merely stand and stare before running away. [*Mock-serious.*] Poor Percy, with his mind on higher things. [*Pause.*] Who am I, though. Someone must know. I must ask my husband. [*Pause.*] To think it is nearly a decade since we arrived here though, baby Sadhbh! I say we, but you'll pardon the flourish. A decade since I… slipped away from it all, down below. [*Pause.*] Mother. Your voracious ghost. What is it now, a decade I said. [*Pause.*] Sometimes I fancy I am back, or never left. But no. [*Pause.*] All best left dead and buried [*Pause.*] It was a dark December when we arrived. All I had wanted was a mountain to huddle under, and there it was, my granite peak by the river, and I somewhere in the folds of its skirt. As a child I would garble the border ballads, bending my vowels this way and that. [*Sings.*] 'As I was walkin all alane, /I heard twa corbies makin a mane.' [*Baby cries.*] Yes, makin a mane, baby Sadhbh! [*Baby cries.*] There, there, perhaps you fancy a bit of breast, why don't I slip down the banks of rose willow herb and feed you by the river. [*Irritated.*] Bother those clegs! Rose willow herb, also known as fireweed. An invasive species, springing up like that along roadsides, leaving no gap unfilled. [*Sound of pushing through high grass. Surprised exclamation.*] Hector! What are you stalking in that outlandish garb? My word though, your tweeds are incomparable!

HECTOR: Aafa fine the day.

AISLING: I don't dispute it. I knew another Hector once. A bull of that name on the Isle of Eigg, left free on the beach to wander where he wished, 'like some fierce tempest that sweeps down upon the sea'. I had the good fortune to view him from behind as he went on his rounds, his lucky bag bouncing with every step.

HECTOR: The wife says I –

AISLING: Spare my blushes, please –

HECTOR: There's a bull in Morrison's field would run you through for sport.

AISLING: But what *are* you doing footering around here, Hector.

HECTOR: I heard tell of an osprey in these parts, come across from Lochter, and thought it might enliven my morning stravaig. But there won't be much fishing for it here.

AISLING: And is that an eagle I see on your fence-post of an evening?

HECTOR: Buzzard. You'll see a buzzard and mistake it for an eagle, but not see an eagle and mistake it for a buzzard.

AISLING: Ah, my greedy gaze, hungry as a hawk for those

visitations. What languorous circles the osprey turns though! Perhaps it might take a lamb – or a baby? Imagine those claws sinking into your sleepsuit baby Sadhbh, and the folds of your thighs! And then to be carried away above Bennachie, who knows where. I have read of a baby in Norway left outside a church for a moment and snatched by an eagle. I picture her sleeping when found, in the eagle's nest.

HECTOR: I had a dog once who –

AISLING *[Oblivious.]*: The ghillies on the estates find the nests and club the poor creatures to death. Knee deep in grouse as they go. I hear the rifles from the forest behind the house and wonder what they can be shooting at: clay pigeons, real pigeons... boom!, it goes, for hours on end. I was at large in the woods one day and so distracted I walked straight into a shooter. I remember the cracked veins on his cheeks as he wheeled round to face me, burgundy capillaries flushed with bloodlust, and his rifle cocked in my face. I held his gaze for a moment, the baby strapped to my chest, and he was gone, a wood-kerne snarling back into the bushes.

HECTOR: I'm getting a powerful smell of slurry.

AISLING: I can't help you there. Though we live surrounded by stench, I'm used to it now, inured to the manure. I doubt if there are small parcels of the stuff in that backpack of yours, Hector, but there are in mine. Bags of dog poo, now, you often see suspended from branches in their black bags, like small dark fruits doomed never to flower.

HECTOR: Pine marten scat is fair boggin.

AISLING: Smelly?

HECTOR: I've a pair at the end of the garden.

AISLING: What admirable creatures. Only descending from their perches to spray, soil, or hunt. Not for them these little courtesies we waste our time on.

Hector: I'll be off so [*whistles to himself as he departs.*]

Aisling: Hector, Hector, don't mistake my musings for unkindness! Oh, but he's gone, back into the banks of fireweed. To be a pine marten of kindness though, emerging from your hideout to dispense small acts of charity, like a nip, to those around you. Poor baby Sadhbh, my kindnesses to you are all too selfish. [*Baby cries.*] Do I do it for you or for my own selfish sake, lying watching over you in the wee small hours. I do it for the greater calm, and me somewhere inside it. [*Sound of distant singing.*] That small symphony of daily song, in which I sometimes raise my voice. [*Singing louder.*] Not in that key though!

Mrs McGillivray [*Sings tunelessly.*]:

> Tho' I pass through the gruesome cleugh,
> Fin' I ken He is near;
> His muckle crook will me defen',
> Sae I ha'e nocht to fear...

Aisling: Mrs McGillivray, what brings you to my slough of despond? Addressing your maker again, on the sweet, sloping banks of the Don?

Mrs McGillivray: That I am, that I am.

Aisling: He is honoured I'm sure. I see He is now a local man, then?

Mrs McGillivray: He has been this gweed while now, he walks these same back roads as you and I. [*Pause.*] And are we not to have the pleasure of seeing you on one of these Sundays?

Aisling: And which kirk's door should I be darkening now? Ah, the call of the faith. Before I came here I no more knew an Episcopalian from a –

Mrs McGillivray: Not Episcopalian. *Not* an –

Aisling: – than I knew an Anabaptist from a Zoroastrian.

Suppose I were to ask you, now, what your thoughts on the real presence are, or taking communion under one or both species? And our saviour's blessed mother, do you offer her latria or merely hyperdulia? These questions worry away at me, I find.

Mrs McGillivray: [*Mutters angrily.*]

Aisling: And our own poor suffering country and its fateful martyrs. Think of the trials of the Earl of Montrose, harried by the Covenanters, then spurned by the king. He was horribly killed and his leg sent to Aberdeen. The left leg, I believe, and his other parts packed off elsewhere. As an example to us. And what of those Covenanters, drowned in their dung in Dunnottar Castle. What would your view be of that class of thing?

Mrs McGillivray: Why is it you talk that way, that... that –

Aisling: What – that what?

Mrs McGillivray: I am the churchgoer, yet you are the one who speaks as though it were 1956, I mean 1596! The Earl of Montrose indeed. [*Mutters.*] And how is baby Sadhbh, named no doubt after one of your heathen serpent goddesses... [*Archly.*] Is there a breath in your body that does not mock the Lord?

Aisling: On the contrary, I –

Mrs McGillivray [*Indignant.*]: I have made pancakes for baby Sadhbh, let me remind you, and scraped their leavings off the church café floor afterwards too, while you go on your way, your head full of folderol and heresy. I do it for –

Aisling: Oh, but your pancakes are exquisite, aren't they baby Sadhbh. [*Baby gurgles.*]

Mrs mcGillivray: ... a higher good.

Aisling: When Christ came to Scotland he was pursued from island to island by his foes. Taking pity on him, some oystercatchers covered him with seaweed until his foes had passed.

I see them stand in the park of a morning, the oystercatchers, the long orange needles of their beaks threading the worms they yank from the earth with such vigour.

MRS MCGILLIVRAY [*Mutters angrily.*]: Oystercatcher... servant of St Brigid... papish mischief...

AISLING: Often, I wondered, talking to my poor lost mother, why it was I the heathen who wittered away about saints while she cried heresy. I was conscious of coming up against a certain... resistance. 'I believe what I believe', she would say. But what do you believe, I would chip away at her. But she couldn't... uncoil enough to say. It is what it is. She was what she was. Whereas I was too busy with my Scotus Eriugena, I mean my Duns Scotus... with the theatre of it all to wonder how much I believed. I have kept the faith to that extent, I suppose. I wish this Scottish Christ of yours well. The place could do with a bit of colour. Just the other day we found a 'Satan''s well – Satan by way of St Anne, I assume, courtesy of some starchy minister purging the landscape of the old saints and their tomfoolery – [*Sharp cry from infant.*]

MRS MCGILLIVRAY [*Impatient.*]: The bairn kens blether when she hears it.

AISLING: It's her Daddy she's missing. [*Sound of pram wheels.*] Off we go!

MRS MCGILLIVRAY: I'll bide here a bittie longer. [*Sotto voce.*] Poor wee bairn, with only those two dafties to...

AISLING: Pancakes tomorrow! But there's a world beyond Mrs McGillivray's prayer book, baby Sadhbh. More things in heaven and earth. [*Sings.*]:

> Thug ho-o, laithill ho-o
> Thug o-ho-ro an àill libh
> Thug ho-o, laithill ho-o
> Seinn o-ho-ro an àill libh.

She means well though. Ah, what can we do but rub along and take each other's sharp edges off with the rubbing. And the slow kiss of your wheels on the tarmac, baby Sadhbh. [*Sound of bus.*] And other passing behemoths. Look, behind us, the half-ten bus! Strange though, why is it stopping? There's no stop, unless it's a… facultative stop, is that the word? And is that old Rona getting off? At her own house too, down that lane. But I know for a fact she's off into town; she volunteers in the shop of a Thursday. Ah, but she has walked to the village first, to catch the bus and… yes, here is she again, with her bag, she must have forgotten it. How kind of the driver! What complex spirals we move in, bumping along the back roads for the chance of a scone at the garden centre or someone's dead mother's shoes in a charity shop. [*Sound of footsteps.*] Someone's dead mother, I say. That word again. [*Pause.*] When I would speak to the doctor she asked if I was escaping the labyrinth, on my walks, or following my mother into its issueless heart. My endless stravaigs. In search of… [*Pause. Cheerier.*] On the off-chance of a brush with a fellow vagrant, there's always that. [*Sound of heavy breathing.*] Would that be you, Eilidh?

EILIDH: Let me just take… these out… what?

AISLING: I notice you jog on the spot rather than stop, why is that?

EILIDH: On the… ? Oh, right! But I'm still going, whether I move or not. [*Pause.*] Did you see that post about the library playdate on Wednesday?

AISLING: What is your Finlay now, still the same age as Percy?

EILIDH: Well he hasn't sped up. And your wee dote here?

AISLING: Oh, it's all new to her, just look at that steely wonder in her bonny blue eyes… poor Sadhbheen, strapped to a baggage like me. [*Pause.*] But nursery though. And all his little friends there, and for playdates too. Percy now… he goes his own way.

EILIDH: Are you still not sending him?

Aisling: 'Too much noise, Mammy.'

Eilidh: We've started Finlay at gym tots too, he's a right demon for it.

Aisling: But he won't be told, Percy I mean, won't be told what to do. Whereas if you put him down in the wood, off he tears like a greyhound until he finds a tree he wants to lie under.

Eilidh: Is that the woods by the skate park?

Aisling: 'There are badgers, Mammy, I saw where they live.'

Eilidh: I find the running such a help though. I was on a personal best passing here yesterday. I wouldn't have stopped if I'd seen you.

Aisling: And today?

Eilidh: You can't expect better every time. [*Pause.*] I mean, I have this coaching app going while I run but...

Aisling: [*To Sadhbh.*] I wonder what I expect from day to day, baby Sadhbh. A little more of the same, neither better nor worse. [*To Eilidh.*] But the muscles on you, Eilidh! Is this oversized belly of mine the anagram of a stomach like yours, do you think? Lurking in there somewhere. But you know all that yourself, I mean with the three of them now. Even with yours having... snapped back into shape.

Eilidh: Himself's parents have been such a help.

Aisling: Sadly for us we... don't have any... The children only have us, I mean, it's us or the orphanage. [*Pause.*]

Eilidh: Lorna's girl is fifteen now and we get her in sometimes. Have you thought about –

Aisling: But he won't have his books from anyone else, no one but us. And what if he needed one and I was off gallivanting...

I owe him that much. And where would I be going anyway, tell me that. I may be here now, but only coming from and going out to see him all over again, isn't that right baby Sadhbh! Not to mention the child's long-suffering father, him too.

EILIDH: My Sandy is gone from seven to seven, I don't know how you manage.

AISLING: Manage?

EILIDH: With having yours round the place. I wouldn't know what to do with mine.

AISLING: But he does have a job, it's not as though he's thrown himself on the mercies of the parish.

EILIDH: Yes, I saw him just yesterday through the café window on my way to yoga, and he was still there when I came back.

AISLING: But the boy though. He will have been under the table, exploring, while his daddy hammered away on his laptop. Your jog though, Eilidh, what of your jog?

EILIDH: Oh, my time is done for!

AISLING: But can't you compensate?

EILIDH: I didn't press the precious button when I stopped. There's no going back now.

AISLING: But can't you just go again? If you pass me a second time I'll slip you the nod and let on this sorry encounter never occurred. [*Pause.*] If only more of life were like that. [*Pause.*] Have you tried running backwards? Granted it's frustrating slowing to a halt, but to go full-tilt in reverse, if not heelstergowdie – arse-over-tit – that must be quite something. The Greeks thought they were moving backwards into the future. If we can see the past it must be in front of us, but the future – where is it? [*Sound of footsteps and muffled leave-taking.*] Oh, but she's gone, and onwards too, to the safe harbour of disappointment. Me too, I hear it calling.

[*Baby starts to cry.*] Not long now, baby Sadhbh, just another bend or two in the road and – [*Sound of laughing.*] But who could that be? Is it the turkeys loose on the road again, or maybe Hamish the cat on his patrols? Don't see anyone… maybe it's lovers in the bushes, fornicating in the long grass. And heedless of a nettle sting on the backside… on the *bahookie* as they cavort. [*Pause.*] But wait, it's gone. [*Pause.*] When I hear voices and see no one I wonder if I am sliding off further into those dangerous reveries, the ones where I think I'm back in… [*Pause.*] No, not that. Shame though to think they might have stopped on my account, the lovers I mean. I remember all that, the mucilaginous pleasures. [*Orotund.*] Mu-ci-la-gi-nous oozings and openings. Now it's all vomit and poo. [*Baby gurgles.*] It is, it is! There's always some orifice or other demanding attention. [*Pause.*] But tramp, tramp, tramp and round the bend and… [*Pause.*] Well can you credit it, but there they are. [*Shouts.*] Arthur, Percy… Percy!

ARTHUR: Is it yourselves? Right so!

AISLING: What a sight, straightening up on me like that from behind the wall, like a corpse sitting up in its coffin. You might have –

PERCY [*interrupting*]: I saw an octagon, Mammy.

AISLING: There you are! I thought you might.

PERCY: It said 'Stop'.

AISLING: Come here to me and give us a kiss, my little man, my sweet little man! [*Noisy embraces.*] Has he been watered and fed? What's this on the pram, on the handle?

ARTHUR: What's… on the what?

AISLING: You've left a pouch there with its top off and now it's smeared all over the cover. Disgusting. Have you no standards. Give me a…

ARTHUR [*Defensive.*]: He… I… he enjoyed his banana. He's been playing in the field while I studied the stone. Those recumbents I told you about, they're –

PERCY [*Singing.*]: 'Incy wincy spider climbed up the waterspout, down came the rain and…'

AISLING: The water bottle is full. I filled it before you left the house and it's still full now. I asked you to –

ARTHUR: No, he's had a –

AISLING: The bottle is full –

ARTHUR: I – he –

AISLING [*Empathic.*]: The bottle is full. [*Pause.*] I say these things and you beat your breast and it happens again the very next day. Who is this woman you pay attention to, I wonder, when she responds to your monologues about castles and mountains and bits of old stone. Not the one scraping scum off the pram! Just look at it all over my fingers.

PERCY: Mammy, mammy, there is a ladybird, it fell off the leaf but I put it back on.

ARTHUR [*To himself.*]: Sweet little mister. Just the other day he was playing on the swings and slides, and when another child approached he didn't like it and threw himself wordlessly to the ground. Then it happened again. Is he mute, asked a woman, does he not speak. Whereas in reality he recites his little songs and poems to me all day long, burbling away to himself. But to whom does he burble, if not his mother and me and the baby. No one, there is no one. Or so it would seem.

AISLING [*Shrieks.*]: Not raspberries on the belly, silly… [*Imitiating him.*] 'Not that!' [*Raspberry noises.*]

ARTHUR: I help and I don't help. Time slows down, speeds up again, I tune in and out. It's a struggle. [*Pause.*] I come here to think about the paleolithic but can't remember last Tuesday, can't remember the child's water bottle. All ancient history. [*Pause. Declamatory.*] 1411, the battle of Harlaw. Before the battle Lachlan Mòr incited the Gaels of Skye with a rousing alphabet song, though his alphabet contained only eighteen of our current twenty-six characters, short-changing the troops of their incitement by a factor of four thirteenths. [*Sings.*] 'As I cam in by Dunnideer and doon by Nether Ha' /There were fifty thoosand heilan man marchin tae Harlaw.' Fifty thousand! I think not. [*Aisling shouts.*] Yes, I have the nappies. [*Pause.*] Oh, but she doesn't want one after all. Just checking on me, maybe. It must be tough for her, having to budget for my little... *longueurs*... my little mental vacancies. Of course the child needs water. He carries his needs around like guilty secrets and never thinks to let me know.

PERCY: Daddy, Daddy.

ARTHUR: Yes, son.

PERCY: There was a lady at the wall.

ARTHUR: Yes, Percy, I know. [*Pause.*] We'll have your pancake later, at the garden centre. [*Pause.*]

PERCY: Not pancake later!

ARTHUR: Oh? You surprise me. Now Percy, when we go home we can have whatever you want...

PERCY [*Defiant.*]: No, we don't like 'whatever you want'! [*Pause.*]

ARTHUR: What? - oh, but he's gone. There *was* a lady at the wall. [*Pause.*] Didn't seem to know where she was going. [*Pause.*] I never fail with the lifted finger when I'm driving, or a subtle wee nod on foot. But let them stop for an actual chat and I'm lost. But she too seemed disoriented. Probably thought the boy here made me more approachable. [*Pause.*] How cheering to pass a stroller and receive that confirmation reserved for a certified fellow human, the face contorted into an impersonation of good humour, and some formula of flim-flam for the impervious child. [*Pause.*] Contrast this with the faces that acknowledge neither child nor parent, hardened against the young and their witless demands. [*Pause.*] But who knows their secret sorrows, maybe years of childlessness and waiting for a child that never come, or came and went. They do right, averting their gaze, rather than stare again into that well of misery. [*Pause.*] But what do I know, who know only joy, joy unbound! [*Pause.*] Ha! How recently there was no little Percy or Sadhbh, and no occasion for mine and a passer-by's eyes to lock in the secret-sharing only parents know, only the slinking past each other, one stepping into the gutter as the other strode by, eyes on a cigarette butt floating into the drain. How quickly I forget. [*Long silence.*] But the lady at the wall, I'm forgetting already. [*Pause. Cheerful again.*] And what of the soup at the garden centre today, baby Sadhbh. [*Gurgling noises.*] That's right, always tomato. I shall stand you on the counter and point you at the 11.15 to Inverness in the station below, the train to Inverness and thence on to the empty zone beyond. I have been on that train and seen it halt at the facultative stop on the vast tundra of the Caithness bog. And yet I saw no one come or go. Strange. Whereas here in the shire now, all is bustle. What a joy to pick up your geranium seeds and compost before embarking in the other direction, if you fancy, for the great metropolis. How are we fixed for slug repellent and weasel traps, I wonder. Why, I fancied I saw a stoat dart across the road, on his way to savage a rabbit. [*Pause.*] It's the neck they go for, always the neck.

PERCY: Daddy, daddy, I did a wee-wee!

ARTHUR: And so you did, on the dandelions. And all by yourself! Let me just give you a wipe with my sleeve.

AISLING: He's asking for his pancake now, so I think we'll be off. I'm sensing your work here is done.

ARTHUR: Yes, my labours are at an end. [*Sound of pram-wheels turning and the bustle of setting off.*] Scrape another footnote out of that maybe, with full chapter to follow by the end of next year. The great work taking shape at last.

PERCY: Carry me, Daddy, give me a carry!

ARTHUR: All right then, up you come. [*Wheezing sound.*] Hup there, and off we go.

AISLING: Did you ring the doctor about your… was it a boil?

ARTHUR: Fungal infection. Of course. Killiecrankie. He told me he was away fly-fishing the next day in Kinlochbervie, or was it Kinlochmoidart, but would leave me a prescription. I picked it up this morning.

AISLING: You surprise me! Not like you to care of yourself.

ARTHUR: Well just last night –

AISLING: Not in front of the children. [*Pause.*]

PERCY: Atchoo!

AISLING: Now look what's happened. You know he doesn't like it when we –

PERCY: Atchoo!

AISLING: Calm down! [*Uses child's voice.*] 'Not with the talking. You can't talk to Daddy.' [*Adult voice again.*] Can't talk to Daddy. [*Pause.*]

ARTHUR: But what would the good doctor say of my chocolate habit. A slab of the stuff forever in my pocket and my fingers ready to snap off a chunk whenever I feel a twinge coming on. Calms it down a bit. Feel it on that inch round my midriff, though, where I can't tuck my shirt in anymore. [*To himself.*] Still, better than the late-night nips of Scotch when everyone else is asleep. One finger, two fingers going down between eleven and twelve with the last wisps of summer daylight. [*Impassioned.*] Cut 'em out! [*Pause.*] Now, wife, if I may – if that's all right with you, Percy. [*Cheerier.*] How goes your novel?

AISLING: My Dickens, you mean?

ARTHUR: Which is it now... *Little Dorrit...*

AISLING: *The Old Curiosity Shop.* I have it here in the pram. Perhaps a page or two in the garden centre...

ARTHUR: And your theory of what it all means?

AISLING: My theory about the villain?

ARTHUR: Remind me.

AISLING: Not Quilp but the grandfather. That's it. Quilp is a brute, he is one of Dickens' music-hall grotesques, gurning and leering and laying waste to all around him. But haven't you read it?

ARTHUR: It sounds a distant horn...

AISLING: But the villain is the grandfather, dragging Nell off to the doom of his fantasy rescue. All the way to Birmingham and its furnaces and 'a hundred strange unearthly noises never heard elsewhere.'

ARTHUR: Why, though. What's your point?

AISLING: I too have trudged. Now, today, I am trudging. But those quixotic treks of my youth, with... [*Affects strange voice.*] 'The man in the church says we may stay for the night. No harm will come to us here. I have reassured him we will be gone in the morning.'

ARTHUR: Still retreading the patrols of your childhood then. When will they let you be? Ah, but who am I to talk, repetitive old ghost-ridden soul that I am. [*Pause.*] But what's that slapping against my face? It's hail – hail in July, Percy and Sadhbh! [*Excited shouts.*]

AISLING [*Resigned.*]: It will pass. It is passing already.

ARTHUR: Washing over us, so sudden and strange on the tongue.

AISLING: Come down from the mountains, maybe it will retreat there.

ARTHUR: There are snow patches up there that never melt. Or almost never. [*Pause.*] But it is not now, in July, they melt, when they do, but the autumn. To cling on all through this insufferable heat, just as summer surrenders its outstretched corpse, and only then expire. And then the next week to start all over again. What rigmarole!

AISLING: Yes, how lucky for us our routines are so laced with joy, the slightest thing about the house –

ARTHUR [*Interrupting.*]: Ouch, ouch! I twanged my string, my… can you get down?

PERCY: Not down, Daddy!

ARTHUR: If you could just… Oh, Percy, I do love to carry you but I'm not always able!

PERCY [*Indignant.*]: You can't say that!

ARTHUR: Why not?

PERCY: You can't say words!

ARTHUR [*Mock-indignant.*]: I can say words, I can!

AISLING: Now now, boys!

ARTHUR: It is the existential refusal. Not just the thing itself but the very language for it. You can't but admire the bloody-mindedness. I'll try him with an iced gem. Never known to fail. [*More wheezing.*] And back in the pram you go. [*Pause. Loud moos nearby.*]

PERCY: There are two bulls in that field, Daddy, they are called Phobos and Deimos.

ARTHUR: Phobos and Deimos, the moons of Mars and the Dalmadilly bulls, filling the valley with their cries. What a balm his planets are. Reading about them the other day we learned that a moon of Neptune, Triton –

AISLING: Must we, must we really.

ARTHUR: – was smashed by asteroids and reformed. It reassembled, just like that. And not once but several times. It made me feel like I too –

AISLING: I see where you're –

ARTHUR: Made me feel like I –

AISLING: Yes, I see where – enough! [*Pause.*] But what's this in the rain-cover? Some kind of... lizard.

ARTHUR: It's my Komodo dragon figurine. I like to keep it about my person.

AISLING: But I saw your precious Komodo dragon just this morning on the bookshelf, beaming down at us murderously.

ARTHUR: Yes you did. [*Pause.*] But not the same one. It, I mean the original one, was there, then baby Sadhbh took and secreted it somewhere. I took advantage of a trip to town last week to replace it. But then I found the original here in the rain-cover. I think I'll just slip it into a jacket pocket, if I may. Maybe swap it round with the other one later. Important to remember which is which, dragon one and dragon two.

AISLING: Have you nothing better to be occupying yourself then? It's well for some.

ARTHUR: But if I don't keep track of these little things I can't attend to the big ones either. They eat away at me like rats in the skull. I feel their little claws tapping against my forehead and wonder how they got there. I feel them now.

AISLING: But you found your dragon, I mean, you got your replacement.

ARTHUR: Yes but suppose I lose it, or lose the replacement. Or forgot which was which. Would it be better, having bought the replacement, to make a clean start? Or having found the original, to dispose of the new one?

AISLING: Or if there had never been a Komodo dragon?

ARTHUR: Well that would be the best of all. But where to stop, once you start down that road. I accumulate to divest, to bring myself closer to the moment when I slough the entire kit and caboodle off, just like that. It will come. Just not yet.

PERCY [*Importunate.*]: Pancake, Mammy, pancake.

AISLING: Yes, Percy, soon. [*To Arthur.*] What a via dolorosa you walk, you and your giant lizards.

ARTHUR: I am a figure of ridicule to you then.

AISLING: You must do what you must.

ARTHUR: But the thousand little connecting strings that hold everything in place, you have no idea. How small, how nearly invisible they are, some of them. Take one away and the whole sorry edifice crumbles. I would take my bed again, and lie there helpless and invertebrate. Enough. On! Did you pay the greengrocer?

AISLING: I did and I didn't. I had the letter in my hand when Mrs MacCaig rang the bell on her bicycle as she passed, and before I knew it baby Sadhbh has popped the letter in the box without a stamp on. She's gone all sporty now. There was a time, baby Sadhbh, I said, when to cycle meant to mount a bicycle and be off on your business, to post-office, Co-op or church. But no more, only the lycraed may now mount and pedal, all others are forbidden.

ARTHUR [*Interrupting, scandalised.*]: Will you leave off about Mrs MacCaig and her infernal get-up? Without a stamp! What were you thinking? What was she thinking?

AISLING: The baby!

Arthur: You, she, yes!

AISLING: I had the wretched thing on the tip of my finger. The stamp, I mean. I still have it now, somewhere in one of my folds.

ARTHUR: Imagine the consternation at the depot. And then when Dougie the postman sees that on his rounds, not least when he sees my name in the top corner. We'll be the talk of the village!

AISLING: I'm sure they can just –

ARTHUR: We have saved the price of a stamp. But at what cost?

AISLING: Could you not straighten it out on your trip to the depot? There was a book, wasn't there, to collect?

ARTHUR: There was a red slip the other day, in amid the junk mail and the piled-up village newsletters. My copy of *Psychopharmacology and Sexual Disorders* at last, perhaps. It's a research interest. Do not imagine I read these things for pleasure. I had hoped to fetch one from the library, but not while this foot and mouth pandemic lasts I can't. But examining the red slip again as I walked I found the depot is open between seven and, not the usual half-past one, but nine, nine in the morning, an hour when even the scholarly caterpillar, eyes moist from self-abuse, should still be a-bed. Our – I mean my trip, is therefore otiose. Bootless, redundant.

AISLING: You had accompanied us only for your book then?

ARTHUR: Yes. [*Pause.*] No. I mean, there were the recumbents and then, there is a bank of wild dog roses in amidst the foxgloves up ahead I'd hoped to –

SADHBH: Gloves. Gloves.

AISLING: That's right, baby Sadhbh, foxgloves! Our monosyllabic little botanist. Where does she get it from?

ARTHUR: Clever child! But is it the flower she loves or the flower's name? The experience of accounting for the world around her one name at a time? It is the latter for me, I find. To name is to have done with, somehow, to exorcise and expunge.

AISLING: 'To have done with' the wild dog rose! Just give it a sniff and be glad can't you. [*Severe.*] You are cold. You were not always so.

ARTHUR: So…?

AISLING: Just 'so'. Not like this. Have you forgotten your ardour when we met, how you used to…?

ARTHUR: Don't!

AISLING: I would be quietly reading my Dickens when you would appear out of nowhere and –

ARTHUR: Don't tell me! I am not what I was. Forgive me. It creeps up on one, or on me at least. Soon I will be fifty. What an old father I am. In no time it is they who will have to worry about my dribbling and soiling myself. [*Meditative.*] And yet look at my dear old parents, still hurling themselves up and down the promenade each morning, and then the cliff walk at weekends, across the sea, in that other life, that other world. But how must we… how must I seem to observers, beyond this little life of ours? When I last gave a lecture I found myself pausing, like a Tube train outside a station, talking and hearing myself talk at once and too bored to carry on. [*Pause.*] Perhaps my audience felt treated to a dramatic pause. But it was more of a… violent nullity, violent but without content, null but asserting itself with animal ferocity. [*Pause.*] Maybe I'm having another one now. [*Pause.*] I clench my fists and wait for my moment of illumination and realize that was it, the moment of waiting, and that nothing will happen. When

I finished my lecture I pressed stop on the recorder and noticed I'd forgotten to turn it on at the start. I am meant to record myself, you see. So I had to do it again, to an empty hall. Sometime towards the end a woman came in early for the next lecture, and sat watching me. I made eye-contact with her, as though – ha! – to explain myself. Yet she sat and listened, offering me her random, unearned attention. I thanked her for it as I left. [*Pause.*] I could not be sure she'd understood. But what had *I*... understood, is that the word? [*Pause.*] But I am lightheaded and irritable. I feel my thoughts drift off into the ether, and me following them as they go. What keeps me tethered to *terra firma*, I wonder. Perhaps these old stones. Significance of mirror imagery on the inscriptions unknown. What was these people's language. Also unknown. What credence should we attach to Diack's hypothesis that, far from a separate language, Brythonic was a form of proto-Gaelic and thus... [*Pause.*] and thus, as we see from the Ogham inscriptions on the Brandsbutt stone, not to speak of the Newton stone with its famed mysterious script... [*Pause.*]

AISLING: But look, Percy, schoolchildren! We have reached the town at least. I can almost smell the skin on my tomato soup. And what a relief to be among civilisation – I mean somewhere I needn't stop and talk to passers-by. Ah, but I've forgotten my blouse, the one that's missing a button. I had hoped to bring it to Miss MacLeod in her wee back room for sewing back on. Without it I feel all agape.

ARTHUR [*Playful.*]: But the poor small breezes that circulate, even in these dog-days of July, what are they for if not to lift a fold or flap and prove we are still lurking underneath? We take our freedoms where we can. [*Pause.*] Now, were I but ten years younger.

AISLING: Oh? [*Impulsive.*] That's come over you all of a sudden. [*Mock-flirtatious.*] How long to the baby-change in the garden centre? Just think of the rattles on the door-handle while we juggled infants and awkward embraces inside. Quick, quick, while the moment lasts! [*Sound of passing cars.*] Bother those buses!

ARTHUR: Oh, I say these things not meaning them. It's all so much idle longing. Pay it no heed. I talk aloud, but think of it as an interior monologue.

AISLING: I am inside your interior monologue then?

ARTHUR: Only in the sense that I am inside yours too. Outside our closed circuit it's –

PERCY: I saw an octagon, Daddy. It said 'stop'.

ARTHUR: Oh but you're doing so well, little mister, so very well. [*Pause.*] Interesting challenge would be to caffeinate your way from one end of town to the other. Note I said caffeine, my boozing days are long done. Starting in the boutique, then proceeding to the Kilted Frog, the railway station café and the garden centre, then on to the art shop and the post office and... am I leaving anywhere out...

PERCY: Daddy's drinking beer!

ARTHUR: Coffee, Percy, coffee.

PERCY: Daddy's drinking coffee!

ARTHUR: You see that mobility buggy outside the Legion from early on most days, I wonder whose it can be. [*Pause. Sound of car engine.*] Maybe some painful case knocked about somewhere sandy and drinking it off now minus a limb or two. Or just a touch of oedema and some varicose veins. [*Pause.*] And there's Murdo sliding into town in his Morgan, and look, the wax jacket too. You see him coming in for *Scottish Field* and maybe a brush for the horses. Old gentility on the march. What a data-base I am, you wouldn't think I spend all that time under my stone at home. And look, it's Monsieur Guillaume pushing his trolley of milk bottles down the street. Adds a touch of panache to the town with his trouser-ends up past his socks like that. Perhaps I can catch his eye, or shout to him that we'll drop in later. After a root around in the charity shops. Sit in the windows with a cappuccino and wonder if the man opposite has finished with the local paper yet.

Cattle show notes most piquant. Stooshie at Locos-Peterhead six-pointer. Time speeds up and slows down again. I drift in and out.

AISLING: Do you see the musician outside the shoe shop, baby Sadhbh? But where is his accordion – what is that contraption he's playing?

ARTHUR: Hurdy-gurdy. [*Sound of Eastern-European folk music.*]

AISLING: See him turn his handle in time to his dirge! A melancholy air from his homeland perhaps. Wonder if they'll make him leave though, now they we've – now that they've – oh but I can't bear to think about that. Must have a rummage and see if I've a pound coin or two to throw to him. What's this in my pocket –

PERCY: Glass flower! Percy wants glass flower!

AISLING: Oh, not the glass flower again! I don't have it, Percy, unless it's right here in – no, it's a washing machine tablet, still in its wrapper. However did that... – but I'm sure your father –

AIRTHUR [*Emphatic.*]: No!

AISLING: Oh dear Percy, we'll just have to – I'm sure we can –

PERCY: Glass flower!

ARTHUR: It's just one of his wee fixations, give it a minute and –

SADHBH: Tomato soup!

AISLING: Again! Getting warmer now.

PERCY: Baby Sadhbh wants soup, Mammy.

ARTHUR: There, you see, he's calmed down already. But coats, hats, nappies, shoes... you try gathering all that up before you leave the house and see if you don't forget something. Coats, hats, nappies, shoes, trousers, replacement trousers and underpants, water bottles, veggie straws, cheesy sticks, pouches (sweet and savoury), squeezy dragon or other toy of the day, reading material currently in favour, sun cream – not to mention one's own items, the small necessaries stashed about one's person but forever at risk of being left behind on kitchen counter, bedside table, or even in the bathroom, left there during a bowel movement, the positively only time of the day one gets to oneself. [*Pause.*] Apologies, when I say 'you try' doing this, I mean 'you' in general, not 'you'-you. [*Pause.*] I am aware of… I know it's… you get my drift… [*Pause.*] Are you all right?

AISLING: What a strange question. You and your 'drift'. I am woken at five by this suckling engine and watch the pair of you snore until seven, but then we get up and you burn the porridge, and here I am walking to the garden centre on an empty stomach with my hair unwashed and a stone in my shoe. Why do you ask?

ARTHUR: Oh just a gesture, can't you permit me my small gestures of solicitude, now and then. [*Pause.*] Once or twice daily, the peck on the cheek, the not entirely hollow expression of care and concern. [*Pause.*] I am not a monster.

AISLING [*Mock-indignant*]: Oh, to be monsters though, you old fool, and not the poor creatures we are! Take my scaly hand a minute, would you, she's jigging around something dreadful.

ARTHUR: Schoolchildren approaching!

AISLING: We'll be mobbed. Have they no concern for the buggy, the thing is the devil itself to manoeuvre.

ARTHUR: And see how they fall into step together like that. The girls all with the same long straight hair and pencil skirts, and the boys with the one strange haircut, what do you call it, an undercut I believe. But look, there's a couple who've broken ranks, sitting together and braving the derision of their peers to touch knees by the war memorial. [*Mutters.*] Don't do it! Stifle those hormones while there's time. A spot of Latin grammar or trigonometry, that should do the trick. [*Surprised.*] But the boy is approaching. He seems to have something to say, you can tell from his look of furious concentration, rather than the usual blank-eyed malevolence of youth.

Boy: Mister, there is a lady wants a word.

Arthur [*Confused.*]: What manner of lady?

Boy: A lady, sitting on the wall, across the street. She asked me to tell you she -

Aisling [*Distressed.*]: What? Where?

Arthur: [*Evasive.*] I see no woman. There was one earlier. She came to the wall. While I was doing my rubbings. I didn't know her, but she seemed to imagine I did. She noticed the smeared pouch on the pram handle and ticked me off, I mean, giving *me* advice, but I… let that pass and…

Aisling: Why didn't you say?

Arthur: I told you I –

Aisling: How could you? How could you?

Arthur: What? What have I done?

Aisling: One minute to be slouching along, you spouting your inanities as per usual, and now this. [*Pause.*] She's getting closer.

Arthur: But I see no one.

Aisling [*Distressed.*]: Have you gone blind as well as astray in your wits? Well, I'm not having it.

Arthur: Should I approach her, if I could just see this mystery woman of yours? What should I say? Let me carry – no, you hold onto… while I…

Aisling: You'll do no such thing. I'm not going back. I believe I had made that clear. I expect you'll be telling me next the voice I hear is my own and not hers.

ARTHUR: Voice, what voice?

AISLING: [*Monotone.*] 'Our misfortunes are the cause.' [*Pause.*] 'We are here and must go on.'

ARTHUR: Tell me what it is you see. I see no one but old Ishbel bent double by her scoliosis.

AISLING: I'm not playing that game anymore. [*Commotion from children. Deadpan again.*] 'Our misfortunes are the cause.'

ARTHUR: What are you saying? You're fretting the children!

AISLING: Advancing straight towards me like that. Oh, there's still time, I mean look at her funereal pace. But she's got me in her sights now, hasn't she, her farcical moment of triumph at last. No doubt she'll have some feeding tips for me, and a card in an envelope for the children. Well, the portable charade can pack itself off on the next train home. Back home! Back nowhere.

ARTHUR [*Panicked.*]: Oh Lord, he's making a break for it. Percy, come back, there are cars! [*Sound of baby crying.*]

AISLING [*Lucid again.*]: Oh, what have I done? Quick, go get him! [*Heavy breathing.*] I could scream. [*Sound of jostling.*]

ARTHUR: There there, Percy! Pancake soon, lovely pancake. [*Sound of Percy's babble, Sadhbh's crying slowly subsiding.*]

AISLING: There there, baby Sadhbh, I'm so sorry. It was nothing really, nothing at all.

ARTHUR: I've got him, I've got him. [*Pause.*] I've got him.

[*Sound of passers-by and traffic. Closing bars of Schubert's 'Der Leiermann', to fade.*]

Note

The Gaelic text sung by Aisling derives from 'Òran eile den Phrionnsa', a welcome for Charles Edward Stuart composed by Alasdair MacMhaighstir Alasdair. Cf. John Lorne Campbell (ed.), *Highland Songs of the Forty-Five* (Scottish Gaelic Texts Society, 1984) and, for pronunciation, Alastair McDonald's version on his 2003 album *Bonnie Prince Charlie*.

SEALL DO BHUAIREADH

KYTHE YER KAUCH

CPSIA information can be obtained
at www.ICGtesting.com
Printed in the USA
LVHW051042040323
740924LV00024B/202

9 781913 642341